4.1.1 ECONOMIC METHODOLOGY AND THE ECONOMIC PROBLEM

The following parts of the syllabus are included in the AQA Year 1 Microeconomics knowledge book

    4.1.1.1 Economic methodology
    4.1.1.2 The nature and purpose of economic activity
    4.1.1.3 Economic resources
    4.1.1.4 Scarcity, choice and the allocation of resources
    4.1.1.5 Production possibility diagrams

4.1.2 INDIVIDUAL ECONOMIC DECISION MAKING

4.1.2.1 CONSUMER BEHAVIOUR *and* 4.1.2.2 IMPERFECT INFORMATION

01 | Define this

Asymmetric information	
Hypothesis	
Imperfect information	
Incentive	
Margin	
Rational behaviour	

Utility	
Marginal utility	
Diminishing marginal utility	

02 | True or False?

Statement	True or False?
Traditional economic theory assumes economic agents are rational	
Utility is a concept that is easy to measure	
Marginal utility is assumed to diminish beyond a certain point	
Diminishing marginal utility may be used to explain the downward sloping nature of the supply curve	
Market failure can result when information is imperfect or asymmetric	
The margin is important in making choices	

03 | 3 2 1!

Give me 3 items from which you derive high levels of utility
1
2
3

Give me 2 problems you experienced when choosing the 3 items you listed above
1
2

Give me the name of 1 economist who suggests a way that utility might be measured
1

04 | Give me 5!

Give me 5 things that a purely rational economic agent is assumed to be able to do
1
2
3
4
5

05 | Complete me!

Fill in the blanks in the passage below, regarding the link between diminishing marginal utility and the demand curve

A demand curve shows the relationship between _____ and quantity demanded. Demand curves slope _____ from left to right. One way to explain the shape of the demand curve is the principle of _____ marginal _____.

Utility, for an economist, is a term that describes the _____ gained from consuming a good or service. In particular, economists are interested in _____ utility. This is the _____ utility enjoyed when _____ more unit of a good or service is _____. In theory, a rational consumer will never pay a price for a good or service that is _____ than the additional satisfaction, or marginal utility, enjoyed. Therefore, price should equate to marginal utility.

Economists assume that as more of a good or service is consumed, the marginal utility gained from consuming additional units will _____. This is because consumers get closer to their point of "_____", where they are fully satisfied. Because marginal utility falls, the price of each additional good or service consumed will also fall. This is why demand curves slope downwards from left to right.

utility	one	downward	satisfaction
consumed	diminishing	marginal	price
satiation	extra	higher	fall

06 | Pros and Cons

Give two advantages and two disadvantages of economic agents choosing to maximise their utility

Advantage 1	Disadvantage 1

Advantage 2	Disadvantage 2

07 | Give me 5!

Give me 5 ways in which there may be imperfect information in an economy

1
2
3
4
5

08 | Tell me!

Tell me why the existence of imperfect information can lead to market failure in an economy

09 | Label Me and Draw Me!

The diagram below shows total utility against total consumption of a product per week. Calculate and draw the associated marginal utility curve. Label the point of satiation (i.e. the point at which no more should be consumed) and the quantity demanded if price is £3 per unit

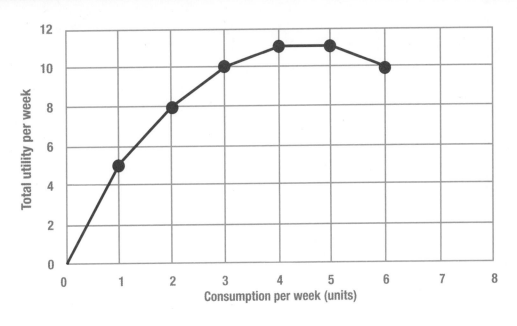

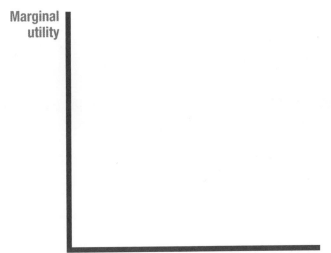

4.1.2.3 ASPECTS OF BEHAVIOURAL ECONOMIC THEORY

01 | Define this

Altruism	

Anchoring	
Availability bias	
Bias	
Bounded rationality	
Bounded self-control	
Heuristics / rules of thumb	
Social norms / herd behaviour	

02 | 3 2 1!

Give me 3 reasons why the behaviour of an economic agent might be irrational
1
2
3

Give me 2 examples of bias
1
2

Give me 1 real world example where irrationality in decision-making is evident
1

03 | True or False?

Statement	True or False?
Behavioural economics questions the assumptions of traditional economic theory	
If information is inaccurate then decisions will be irrational	
A decision that is regretted is one that is irrational	
Behavioural economics can provide an explanation for asset price bubbles	
It is likely that all economic agents are irrational to an extent	
The existence of irrationality means that traditional theory is redundant	
The more complex the information, the more likely it is that rationality will be bounded	
Altruism is about making the most efficient decisions	

04 | Give me 5!

Give me the names of 5 economists who are well known in the field of behavioural economics, and give an example of their work/research
1
2
3
4
5

05 | 3 2 1!

Give me 3 examples of anchoring
1
2
3

Give me 2 examples of economic actions related to altruism
1
2

Give me 1 example of the availability bias in action
1

06 | Tell me!

Tell me at least 5 ways in which decisions you have made today might have been influenced by biases

4.1.2.4   BEHAVIOURAL ECONOMICS AND ECONOMIC POLICY

01 | Define this

Choice architecture	
Framing	
Anchoring	
Nudge	
Default choice	

Mandated choice	
Restricted choice	

02 | 3 2 1!

Give me 3 causes of market failure

1

2

3

Give me 2 examples of market failure where behavioural economic policies might be particularly effective in solving the problem

1

2

Give me 1 type of market failure where behavioural policies are unlikely to work

1

03 | Give me 5!

Give me 5 real world examples of behavioural nudges

1

2

3

4

5

04 | Pros and Cons

Give two advantages and two disadvantages of using behavioural policies to reduce demand for and consumption of a demerit good

Advantage 1	Disadvantage 1

Advantage 2	Disadvantage 2

05 | Give me 5!

1 Give me an example of a market failure being tackled by altering the default choice

2 Give an example of choice architecture being used in a way that might lead to an irrational consumer decision

3 Give me an example of a negative externality being tackled by using a nudge

4 Give me an example of framing that should improve economic efficiency

5 Give me an example of a positive externality being tackled by using a nudge

For each of the behavioural interventions outlined below, suggest one reason why the intervention should be effective and one reason why it might not be effective

	Effective	Ineffective
1 A school canteen placing fruit in bowls at the front of the counter, and putting cake on a plate under a cover at the back of the counter, in order to improve healthy eating		
2 The UK government changing its policy on organ donation, so that when you sign up to get a driving licence you are automatically enrolled in the organ donation scheme and must actively opt-out if you do not want to take part		
3 A notice being placed above bins in a town-centre, asking people to think carefully about which bin (general waste, recycling or compost) to select for their rubbish		

4.1.3 PRICE DETERMINATION IN A COMPETITIVE MARKET

The following parts of the syllabus are included in the AQA Year 1 Microeconomics knowledge book

    4.1.3.1 The determinants of the demand for goods and services
    4.1.3.2 Price, income and cross elasticities of demand
    4.1.3.3 The determinants of the supply of goods and services
    4.1.3.4 Price elasticity of supply
    4.1.3.5 The determination of equilibrium market prices
    4.1.3.6 The interrelationship between markets

4.1.4 PRODUCTION, COSTS AND REVENUE

The following parts of the syllabus are included in the AQA Year 1 Microeconomics knowledge book

    4.1.4.1 Production and productivity
    4.1.4.2 Specialisation, division of labour and exchange

01 | Define this

Short run	
Long run	
Average Returns	
Marginal Returns	
Total Returns	
Law of diminishing returns	
Returns to scale	
Increasing returns to scale	
Decreasing returns to scale	
Constant returns to scale	

02 | True or False?

Statement	True or False?
The law of diminishing marginal returns is a short run production theory, whereas returns to scale is a long run production theory	
Both the law of diminishing returns and returns to scale concepts explain the relationship between inputs and outputs	

If marginal returns are above average returns, then average returns will be falling

Diminishing marginal returns set in when marginal returns are zero

The law of diminishing returns and returns to scale have implications for the costs of production

Diminishing marginal returns are inevitable because eventually the benefits from specialisation lessen

Diminishing marginal returns occur when all factors of production are variable

03 | Give me 5!

Give me 5 benefits of specialisation for a firm
1
2
3
4
5

04 | 3 2 1!

Give me 3 possible causes of increasing returns to scale
1
2
3

Give me 2 possible reasons for decreasing returns to scale
1
2

Give me 1 industry that is likely to experience increasing returns to scale
1

05 | Give me 5!

Give me 5 specific examples of increasing returns to scale that an airline might benefit from
1
2
3
4
5

06 | Give me 3!

Give me 3 specific examples of decreasing returns to scale that a supermarket chain might suffer
1
2
3

07 | Label me!

The diagram below shows short run product information. Label the horizontal axes, the un-named curve and identify the point at which diminishing marginal returns set in

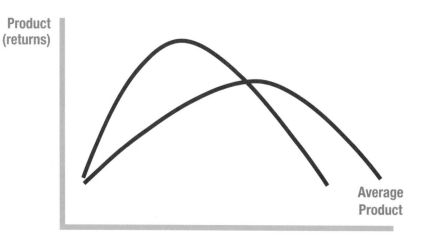

08 | Pros and Cons

Give two advantages and two disadvantages to a firm of experiencing increasing returns to scale

Advantage 1	Disadvantage 1

Advantage 2	Disadvantage 2

4.1.4.4   COSTS OF PRODUCTION

01 | Define this

Average cost	
Factor inputs	
Factor prices	
Fixed cost	
Long-run cost	
Marginal cost	
Production	

Productivity	
Short-run cost	
Total cost	
Variable cost	

02 | 3 2 1!

Give me 3 examples of variable costs
1
2
3

Give me 2 examples of fixed costs
1
2

Give me 1 example of a quasi-fixed cost
1

03 | True or False?

Statement	True or False?
The law of diminishing marginal returns explains the shape of the marginal cost curve	
The marginal cost curve explains the shape of the average variable cost curve	
The average fixed cost curve is upward sloping	

AVC + ATC = AFC

When MC<AC then AC will be rising

MC cuts both the AVC and ATC at their lowest points

Factor prices and productivity affect a firm's choice of factor inputs

An increase in the price of capital is likely to reduce the capital:labour ratio

04 | Give me 5!

Give me 5 factors that explain the shape and position of the short run cost curves
1
2
3
4
5

05 | Draw me!

Draw a diagram to represent each of the following concepts	
Average Cost and Marginal Cost in the Short Run	Average Cost in the Long Run

Costs

Output

Costs

Output

	Average Fixed Cost		Average Variable Cost and Average Total Cost

Costs

Output

Costs

Output

06 | Tell me!

Tell me the formula, or tell me how you would calculate, each of the following			
Total Cost		Variable Cost	
Fixed Cost		Average Total Cost	
Average Fixed Cost		Average Variable Cost	
Marginal Cost			

4.1.4.5   ECONOMIES AND DISECONOMIES OF SCALE

01 | Define this

Barriers to entry	
External economies of scale	
Diseconomies of scale	

Internal economy of scale	
Minimum efficient scale	
Network economies of scale	
Optimal scale of production	

02 | **True or False?**

Statement	True or False?
Economies and diseconomies of scale are shown on a long-run average cost (LRAC) curve	
LRAC curves are always "U" shaped	
Technical economies are an example of external economies of scale	
Significant economies of scale increase the barriers to entry in an industry	
Minimum efficient scale has no impact on market structure	

03 | **3 2 1!**

Give me 3 causes of an industry having a high minimum efficient scale
1
2
3

Give me 2 ways in which a high minimum efficient scale could affect industry structure
1
2

Give me 1 example of an industry that is likely to have a high minimum efficient scale

1

04 | Draw me and Label me!

Draw a diagram to show economies and diseconomies of scale in the long run

On the diagram below, label the minimum efficient scale, and indicate the entire range of output at which there are constant returns to scale

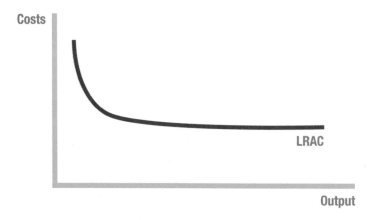

Adapt the diagram below to show the impact of external economies of scale on average costs

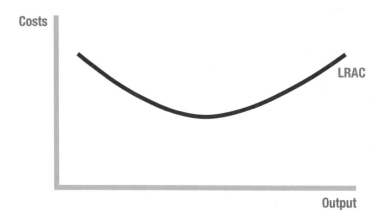

Tell me what each of the following types of economy of scale means, and then give an example of each

	Explanation	Example
Financial economies		
Purchasing economies		
Technical economies		
Managerial economies		
Marketing economies		

4.1.4.6 MARGINAL, AVERAGE AND TOTAL REVENUE

01 | **Define this**

Total revenue	
Marginal revenue	
Average revenue	
Demand curve	

02 | True or False?

Statement	True or False?
Total revenue = price x quantity	
The demand curve is the same as the marginal revenue curve	
Average revenue = price per unit = total revenue/output	
If the AR curve is downward sloping then MR > AR	
Marginal revenue = the change in revenue from selling one extra unit of output	

03 | Give the Formula!

Total revenue	
Average revenue	
Marginal revenue	

04 | Calculate!

For the demand schedule given below, calculate total revenue, average revenue, and marginal revenue				
Price (£)	Quantity Demanded	Total Revenue	Marginal Revenue	Average Revenue
5.00	10			
4.50	15			
4.00	20			
3.50	25			
3.00	30			
2.50	35			
2.00	40			
1.50	45			
1.0	50			
0.5	55			

The diagram below shows a demand curve. This is also known as the average revenue curve.
  i)   Draw the accompanying marginal revenue curve
  ii)   Label the axes
  iii)   Label the sections of the demand curve which are price elastic and price inelastic
  iv)   Label the point of unitary price elasticity of demand

Average Revenue
(AR = D)

06 | **3 2 1!**

Give me 3 reasons why a business might face relatively price inelastic demand

1

2

3

Give me 2 possible impacts for a firm if it has price inelastic demand

1

2

Give me 1 strategy a firm might use to make demand more price inelastic

1

07 | Tell me!

Tell me why, for a downwards sloping demand curve, marginal revenue is always less than average

Tell me why, for a perfectly elastic (i.e. horizontal) demand curve, marginal revenue is equal to average revenue

08 | Draw me!

For each of the average revenue curves drawn below, draw the associated total revenue curve

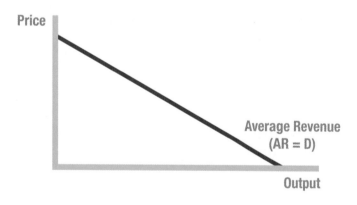

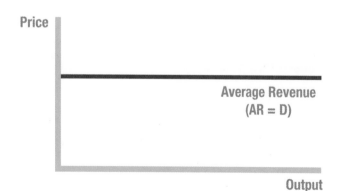

4.1.4.7 PROFIT

01 | Define this

Abnormal (supernormal) profit	
Normal profit	
Profit	
Sub-normal profit	

02 | Give me 5!

Give me 5 roles of profit in a market economy
1
2
3
4
5

03 | Find out!

Carry out research to
  i)   find 2 examples of businesses that have experienced sub-normal profits or losses, and outline the reasons why
  ii) find 2 examples of businesses that have experienced high supernormal profits, and outline the reasons why

Sub-normal profit or loss-making business example 1:	Reasons:

NOT LICENSED FOR REPRODUCTION - PLEASE DO NOT COPY THIS BOOKLET **www.tutor2u.net** 27

Sub-normal profit or loss-making business example 2:	Reasons:
Abnormal profit business example 1:	Reasons:
Abnormal profit business example 2:	Reasons:

04 | Label Me!

On the diagrams below indicate all of the areas representing supernormal profit, and all the areas representing a loss. Mark the levels of output at which normal profit is earned

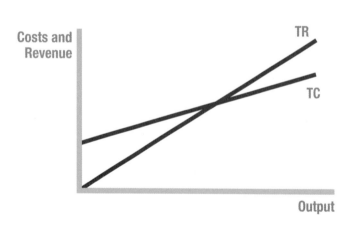

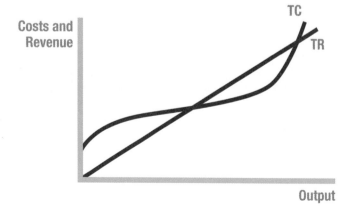

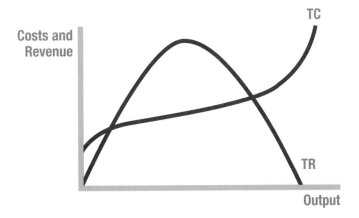

05 | Complete me!

Complete the passage on profits, using the words provided

In simple terms, profit means total revenue minus total _____. For an economist, profit is the reward for providing the _____ factor of production. Usually, the _____ the market, the greater the level of profit that an entrepreneur will seek, in order to be _____ to join the market.

Economists distinguish between different types of profit. Normal profit is the _____ profit required to keep all of a business's factors of production in their _____ use. In other words, it is just enough profit for that business to keep on _____. This is not the same as what _____ might call the break-even point of a business. This is because economists also include _____ cost when they are working out their total costs of production i.e. total cost equals the _____ costs of production such as raw materials and energy bills, as well as other fixed costs such as _____ and also the opportunity cost of what that firm's factors of production could be used for in their next-best _____ use.

Supernormal, or _____, profit is any profit earned by a business _____ its level of normal profit. Rising _____ in an industry tends to cause supernormal profit to be reduced, or _____.

Subnormal profit exists when total _____ is less than total cost. However, because economists include opportunity cost in their calculation of _____ cost, it could be the case that the business is still earning _____ profit rather than making a loss. When a firm earns subnormal profit, economists assume that this firm will leave the industry in the _____ run.

riskier	minimum	direct	cost
salaries	enterprise	accountants	some
opportunity	above	competition	incentivised
revenue	current	total	alternative
appropriated	long	producing	abnormal

01 | Define this

Creative destruction	
Dynamic efficiency	
Efficiency	
Innovation	
Invention	
Market structure	
Productivity	
Technological change	

02 | True or False?

Statement	True or False?
Technological change can affect methods of production, productivity, costs and efficiency	
Technological change can lead to process and/or product innovation	
Technological change always lowers barriers to entry	
Technological change can lead to the process of creative destruction	
It is necessarily a bad thing when a business shuts down	
Technological change always improves efficiency	
Technological change is always rapid	
Technological change can influence the structure of markets	

03 | Give me 5!

Give me 5 real world examples of technological change that have significantly impacted on market structures
1
2
3
4
5

04 | 3 2 1!

Give me 3 ways in which technological change can affect market structure
1
2
3

Give me 2 impacts of technological change affecting market structure
1
2

Give me the name of 1 economist who discussed creative destruction
1

05 | Give me 5 more!

Give me 5 examples of creative destruction
1

2	
3	
4	
5	

06 | Pros and Cons

Give two advantages and two disadvantages of creative destruction for an economy

Advantage 1	Disadvantage 1
Advantage 2	Disadvantage 2

07 | Give me 3!

Give me 3 examples of innovation
1
2
3

Give me 3 examples of invention
1
2
3

Tell me why technological change can improve allocative efficiency

Tell me why technological change could lower a firm's fixed costs

4.1.5 PERFECT COMPETITION, IMPERFECTLY COMPETITIVE MARKETS AND MONOPOLY

4.1.5.1 MARKET STRUCTURES

01 | Define this

Market structure	
Duopoly	
Monopolistic competition	
Monopoly	
Pure monopoly	
Oligopoly	

Perfect competition	
Contestable market	
Spectrum of competition	

02 | Give me 5!

Give me 5 factors that can be used to distinguish between different market structures
1
2
3
4
5

4.1.5.2   THE OBJECTIVES OF FIRMS

01 | True or False?

Statement	True or False?
The traditional theory of the firm assumes that firms will aim to maximise profit	
The size of a business may mean there is a divorce of ownership from control	
Stakeholders are likely to have broadly similar objectives	
Shareholders are least likely to be interested in maximising profit	
Objectives other profit maximising include survival, growth, quality, maximising revenue and increasing market share	
The objectives of a firm will affect their conduct and performance	

Give me 3 reasons why a firm may adopt objectives other than profit maximisation

1

2

3

Give me 2 consequences of a firm choosing to adopt a different objective to profit maximisation

1

2

Give me 1 real world example of a business adopting a different objective

1

03 | **Draw Me!**

Draw a diagram showing the MR and MC curves of a firm, and label the profit maximising level of output

04 | **Tell me!**

Tell me why profit is maximised when marginal revenue is equal to marginal cost

05 | Give the Formula!

For each of the alternative objectives given below, state the relevant formula (if appropriate) and then explain why that objective is achieved at the point given by the formula

	Formula	Justification
Sales revenue maximisation		
Sales volume maximisation		
Productive efficiency		
Allocative efficiency		
Normal profit		

06 | Label me!

The diagram below represents a firm in imperfect competition. Label the following levels of output – (i) profit maximisation (ii) revenue maximisation (iii) normal profit and (iv) the range of output between which satisficing may occur

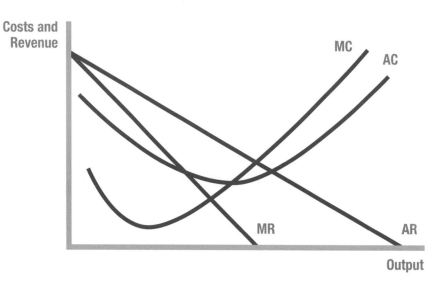

07 | Tell me!

Tell me some possible objectives that each of the following stakeholders might have. Assume that the business concerned is a large chocolate manufacturer

Manager	
Shareholder	
Supplier	
Employee	
Local resident	
Creditors	
Trade union	
Government	

08 | Complete me!

Complete the passage on the divorce of ownership and control, using the words provided

The problem of the divorce of ownership and control is often also called the _____ - agent problem, or the agency problem. It exists because owners (e.g. _____) tend to have different _____ to the day-to-day managers. For example, shareholders are often particularly interested in a firm's _____ because this will affect the value of _____ that they earn each year, as well as the value of their _____. On the other hand, managers may be more concerned with meeting _____ targets or ensuring that employees are well _____. Because the shareholders are not present very much of the time, there is therefore an _____ gap. This gap can be widened further because many shareholders are highly _____ investors, for example large institutions such as _____ funds or insurance companies.

Many businesses are aware of the problems caused by the divorce of ownership from control, and have put into place some strategies for preventing it from happening. One such approach is known as the _____ share-ownership scheme, or partnership model, in which employees are given shares in addition to their pay so that they also have an interest in improving company profits and share prices. However, this can sometimes lead to _____-termism and greater incentive to carry out _____ or undesirable actions to raise share _____. An alternative strategy would be to offer managers much longer term employment _____, so that they are focused on the longer term survival of the business rather than short-term "firefighting".

shareholders	dividends	employee	shares
short	information	sales	profit
principal	prices	pension	illegal
passive	contracts	objectives	motivated

09 | Pros and Cons

Give two advantages and two disadvantages to a firm of having profit maximisation as their objective	
Advantage 1	Disadvantage 1
Advantage 2	Disadvantage 2

4.1.5.3 PERFECT COMPETITION

01 | Define this

Homogenous	
Benchmark	
Price taker	

Short run	
Long run	
Perfect knowledge	

02 | Give me 5!

Give me 5 assumptions of perfect competition
1
2
3
4
5

03 | True or False?

Statement	True or False?
The assumptions of perfect competition mean that individual firms are price takers	
Given certain assumptions (such as an absence of externalities) perfect competition will result in an efficient allocation of resources	
There are a number of real world examples of perfect competition	
In the short run, firms in perfect competition may earn abnormal profit	
Abnormal profit acts as a signal for new firms to enter the market in the long run	
Barriers to entry make it difficult for new firms to enter	
The long run equilibrium condition in perfect competition is normal profit	

04 | 3 2 1!

Give me 3 reasons why real-world markets will not be perfectly competitive

1

2

3

Give me 2 impacts of real-world markets not being perfectly competitive

1

2

Give me 1 technological change that might make markets closer to perfect competition

1

05 | Draw Me!

Draw a diagram to show a firm in perfect competition earning below normal profit in the short run

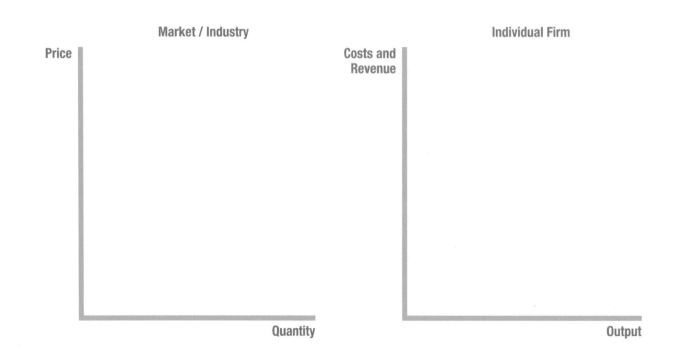

Market / Industry

Individual Firm

Price

Costs and
Revenue

Quantity

Output

Now adapt the diagram on the previous page to show how equilibrium is achieved in the long run. Explain the process below:

06 | Draw Me!

Draw a diagram to show a firm in perfect competition earning abnormal profit in the short run

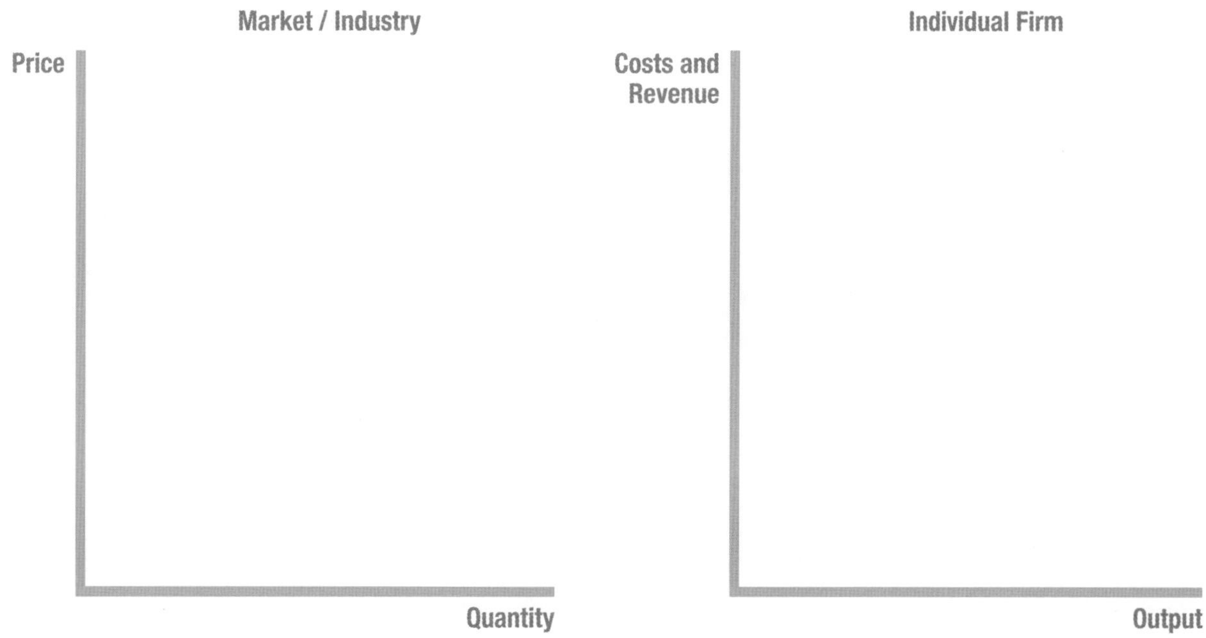

Market / Industry

Price

Quantity

Individual Firm

Costs and Revenue

Output

Now adapt the diagram above to show how equilibrium is achieved in the long run. Explain the process of adjustment below:

Tell me, using the diagrams below, about the efficiency of firms in perfect competition

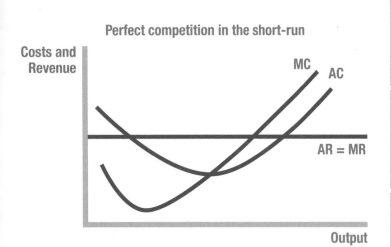

Perfect competition in the short-run

Productive efficiency:

Allocative efficiency:

Dynamic efficiency:

Summary:

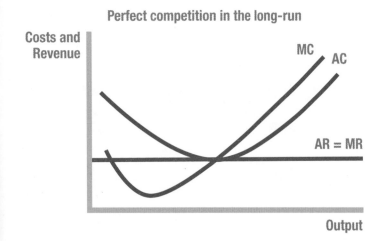

Perfect competition in the long-run

Productive efficiency:

Allocative efficiency:

Dynamic efficiency:

08 | Pros and Cons

Give two advantages and two disadvantages for firms and/or consumers of a perfectly competitive market structure

Advantage 1	Disadvantage 1

Advantage 2	Disadvantage 2

4.1.5.4 MONOPOLISTIC COMPETITION

01 | Define this

Product differentiation	
Price makers	
Brand loyalty	
Non-price competition	

02 | 3 2 1!

Give me 3 ways in which monopolistic competition is different to perfect competition

1

2

3

Give me 2 outcomes in a monopolistically competitive market structure
1
2

Give me 1 way in which a firm in monopolistic competition might try and increase their market share
1

03 | Give me 5!

Give me 5 real world examples of monopolistic competition
1
2
3
4
5

04 | True or False?

Statement	True or False?
Monopolistic competition is a more realistic model of market structure than perfect competition	
Firms are price takers in monopolistic competition	
The industry concentration ratio is low in monopolistic competition	
Product differentiation means firms face a downward facing demand curve	
The demand curve in monopolistic competition is price inelastic	
Barriers to entry and exit are high	
Firms in monopolistic competition earn normal profit in the long run	

05 | Pros and Cons

Advantage 1	Disadvantage 1

Advantage 2	Disadvantage 2

06 | Label me!

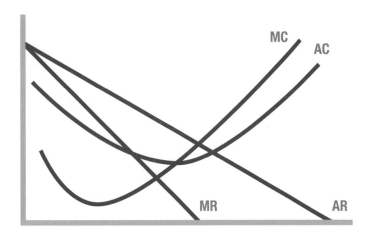

Now draw a diagram below to show what happens to this firm in the long run

Explain the process by which the firm adjusts from the short run to the long run equilibrium

07 | Give me 5!

Give me 5 examples of non-price competition that could be used by a monopolistically competitive firm
1
2

3	
4	
5	

4.1.5.5 OLIGOPOLY

01 | Define this

Concentration ratio	
Collusion	
Cooperation	
Cartel	
Price leadership	
Interdependence	
Oligopoly	
Product differentiation	
Price agreement	

Price war	
Joint profits	

02 | 3 2 1!

Give me 3 factors likely to increase the chances of a market structure being oligopolistic
1
2
3

Give me 2 impacts on market participants of being in an oligopolistic market
1
2

Give me 1 example of non-price competition that could be used by a firm in an oligopoly
1

03 | Give me 5!

Give me 5 real world examples of oligopolistic industries
1
2
3
4
5

04 | True or False?

Statement	True or False?
Oligopolistic markets are all similar in terms of number of firms, product differentiation and ease of entry	
Oligopolies can be collusive or non-collusive	
Cooperation over the development of a product is illegal	
The kinked demand curve model is the only model of oligopoly	
Interdependence and the consequent uncertainty is central in explaining this market structure	

05 | Draw Me!

Draw a fully-labelled diagram to show a kinked demand curve of a profit maximising firm where price stability is likely

06 | Give me 5 more!

Give me 5 real world examples of collusion
1
2
3
4
5

07 | Give me yet another 5!

Give me 5 real world examples of cooperation

1

2

3

4

5

08 | Pros and Cons

Give two advantages and two disadvantages of Oligopoly for consumers

Advantage 1	Disadvantage 1
Advantage 2	Disadvantage 2

Give two advantages and two disadvantages of Oligopoly for the wider economy

Advantage 1	Disadvantage 1
Advantage 2	Disadvantage 2

Tell me how to calculate a concentration ratio

Tell me the 3-firm concentration ratio in each of the following examples

Mortgage lenders (UK) in 2021, by market share		Calculation:
Lloyds Banking Group	18.14%	
Natwest Group	11.71%	
Nationwide BS	11.49%	
Santander UK	10.77%	
Barclays	10.71%	
HSBC Bank	8.86%	
Coventry BS	3.28%	
Yorkshire BS	3.24%	

New car sales market share, UK 2022		Calculation:
Volkswagen	8.17%	
Ford	7.86%	
Audi	6.82%	
BMW	6.73%	
Toyota	6.33%	
Kia	6.21%	
Vauxhall	5.19%	
Mercedes-Benz	5.01%	
Hyundai	4.98%	
Nissan	4.75%	

10 | What's the difference?

Collusive and non-collusive oligopoly?	
Cooperation and collusion?	
Overt and tacit collusion?	

11 | Complete me!

Complete the passage below on the kinked demand curve, using the terms provided

The _____ demand curve model is one way of illustrating how firms in an _____ are interdependent in terms of their _____ decisions. The model is only relevant to firms that tend to have relatively _____ goods / services rather than competing heavily in non-price ways.

The model suggests that there is a _____ price that firms are unlikely to deviate away from. This is because if they raise their _____ then consumers will simply buy from their _____. Therefore, an increase in the firm's price will lead to a _____ than proportionate fall in quantity demanded. This is why the upper section of the kinked demand curve is drawn as relatively price _____. Conversely, a fall in the firm's price will trigger price _____ and perhaps even a price _____. The firm will gain very few additional customers, because all firms have copied. Therefore, a fall in the firm's price will lead to a _____ than proportionate increase in quantity demanded and so the lower section of the kinked demand curve is drawn as relatively price _____.

The kinked demand curve model is not without its criticisms, though. For example, in many oligopolies we may see the existence of price _____ or tacit collusion – an increase in the price by one firm is copied by others because they see an opportunity to earn more _____, especially if the good or service in question is a _____. Furthermore, there is nothing in the theory underpinning the model that suggests how the _____ price comes about in the first place; the model is _____ rather than dynamic. Also, many firms in an oligopoly compete in terms of ____-price competition, and this cannot be accounted for by the kinked demand curve. Finally, some oligopolistic firms selling relatively homogeneous products will engage

in _____.

stable	profit	less	more
competition	stable	inelastic	competitors
pricing	war	price	oligopoly
necessity	elastic	homogeneous	leadership
static	kinked	non	collusion

12 | Give me 2!

Give 2 factors that might influence each of the behaviours below in an oligopolistic firm		
	Factor 1	Factor 2
Price		
Output		
Investment		
Expenditure on R&D		
Expenditure on advertising		

13 | 5 4 3 2 1!

Give me 5 conditions that need to exist in a market for collusion to be likely
1
2
3
4
5

Give me 4 possible policies that a government could use to reduce the risk of collusion occurring
1
2
3
4

Give me 3 reasons why collusive agreements between firms may break-down without government intervention
1
2
3

Give me 2 reasons why collusion may be bad for consumers
1
2

Give me 1 reason why collusion may actually be good for consumers
1

4.1.5.6   MONOPOLY AND MONOPOLY POWER

01 | Define this

Monopoly	
Monopoly power	

Price maker	
Product differentiation	
Abnormal profit	
Consumer surplus	
Barriers to entry	

02 | True or False?

Statement	True or False?
There are many real-world examples of true monopoly	
All monopolists have monopoly power	
All firms with monopoly power are monopolists	
The kinked demand curve model is the only model of oligopoly	
Firms in oligopoly and monopolistically competitive markets are price makers and have varying degrees of monopoly power	

03 | 3 2 1!

Give me 3 differences between monopoly and monopolistic competition
1
2
3

Give me 2 factors that increase the likelihood of a firm operating as a monopoly
1
2

Give me 1 example of a natural monopoly
1

04 | Draw Me!

Draw a costs and revenue diagram to show a profit maximising monopolist, making sure that you label the profit maximising level of output, and indicate the area of abnormal profit

05 | Give me 5!

Give me 5 examples of real world businesses that are considered to be monopolies. Note down whether you think they are local monopolies, national monopolies, or global monopolies
1
2
3

4	
5	

06 | **Pros and Cons**

Give two advantages and two disadvantages of monopoly for consumers

Advantage 1	Disadvantage 1
Advantage 2	**Disadvantage 2**

Give two advantages and two disadvantages of monopoly for the monopolist themselves

Advantage 1	Disadvantage 1
Advantage 2	**Disadvantage 2**

Give two advantages and two disadvantages of monopoly for their suppliers

Advantage 1	Disadvantage 1

Advantage 2	Disadvantage 2

Give two advantages and two disadvantages of monopoly for the wider economy

Advantage 1	Disadvantage 1

Advantage 2	Disadvantage 2

07 | Give me 5!

Give me 5 factors that can influence the degree of monopoly power

1
2
3
4
5

Using the diagram below, tell me about the efficiency of monopolies

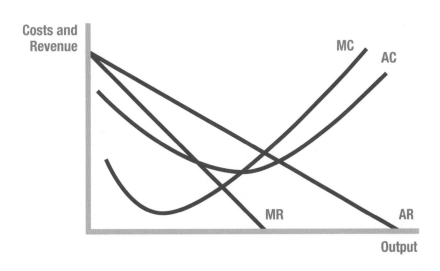

Why a monopoly could be considered productively inefficient	
Why a monopoly could be considered productively efficient	
Why a monopoly could be considered allocatively inefficient	
Why a monopoly could be considered allocatively efficient	
Why a monopoly could be considered dynamically efficient	
Why a monopoly could be considered dynamically inefficient	

01 | Define this

Price discrimination	
Product differentiation	
First degree price discrimination	
Second degree price discrimination	
Third degree price discrimination	
Market segmentation	
Seepage / arbitrage	
Price elasticity of demand	

02 | Give me 5!

Give me 5 real world examples of price discrimination, making sure you note down the degree of price discrimination observed
1
2
3

4
5

03 | 3 2 1!

Give me 3 factors necessary for third-degree price discrimination to be possible
1
2
3

Give me 2 reasons why firms might choose to price discriminate
1
2

Give me 1 benefit to consumers of price discrimination
1

04 | True or False?

Statement	True or False?
Price discrimination has impacts on both consumers and producers	
Consumers have nothing to gain from price discrimination	
One reason railcards need to be shown on trains is to prevent seepage / arbitrage between different market segments	
Technological progress increases the possibilities for price discrimination	
There have been examples of competition authorities banning price discrimination in some circumstances	

05 | Draw me!

Draw a diagram (or diagrams) to show how third-degree price discrimination might work to increase a firm's profits

06 | Label me!

The diagram below shows a firm not currently price discriminating, and profit maximising at P1Q1. Label the profit maximising level of output if the firm now decides to use perfect (first degree) price discrimination

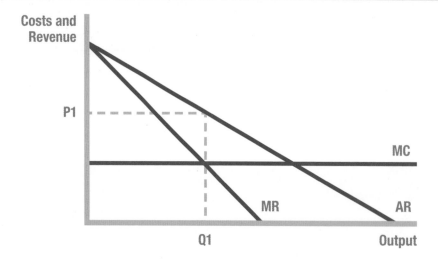

07 | Pros and Cons

Give two advantages and two disadvantages of price discrimination for producers

Advantage 1	Disadvantage 1

Advantage 2	Disadvantage 2

Give two advantages and two disadvantages of price discrimination for consumers	
Advantage 1	Disadvantage 1
Advantage 2	Disadvantage 2

4.1.5.8 THE DYNAMICS OF COMPETITION AND COMPETITIVE MARKET PROCESSES

01 | Define this

Competitive market process	
Creative destruction	
Monopoly power	
Barriers to entry	

02 | True or False?

Statement	True or False?
If firms are making large profits there will be an incentive over time for other firms to attempt to enter the market	
Technological innovation provides a way by which existing barriers to entry might be overcome	
There are both short run and long run benefits from competition	
Keynes is the economist known for developing the concept of "creative destruction"	
Creative destruction is a fundamental way in which competition operates in a market economy	
The competitive market process is static rather than dynamic	

03 | 3 2 1!

Give me 3 ways in which firms might compete other than by changing the price
1
2
3

Give me 2 possible impacts on consumers of firms using non-price competition
1
2

Give me 1 real world example of a firm using non-price competition
1

04 | **Pros and Cons**

Give two advantages and two disadvantages of the competitive market process for firms –
try to give 1 short-run and 1 long-run aspect of each

Advantage 1	Disadvantage 1

Advantage 2	Disadvantage 2

Give two advantages and two disadvantages of the competitive market process for consumers

Advantage 1	Disadvantage 1

Advantage 2	Disadvantage 2

4.1.5.9 CONTESTABLE AND NON-CONTESTABLE MARKETS

01 | **Define this**

Contestable	
Sunk cost	

Incumbent	
Hit and run competition	
Limit pricing	

02 | Give me 5!

Give me 5 aspects of a contestable market
1
2
3
4
5

03 | True or False?

Statement	True or False?
In contestable market theory, the number of firms currently in an industry is irrelevant to profit and performance	
Pure contestability is far more likely than perfect competition	
In a purely contestable market, firms will earn only normal profit even if there is only one incumbent firm	
Technological change always increases the contestability of a market	
If consumers have strong brand loyalty, market contestability will be high	

04 | 3 2 1!

Give me 3 factors likely to increase the contestability of an industry

1
2
3

Give me 2 impacts on consumers of increased contestability in a market

1
2

Give me 1 economist known for the theory of contestability

1

05 | Give me 3!

Give me 3 policies a government might use to increase contestability in a market

1
2
3

06 | Give me 4!

Give me 4 examples of UK markets that have become more contestable

1
2
3
4

07 | Label me!

The diagram below shows a profit maximising firm.
Label where a firm would have an incentive to operate instead if the market is highly contestable

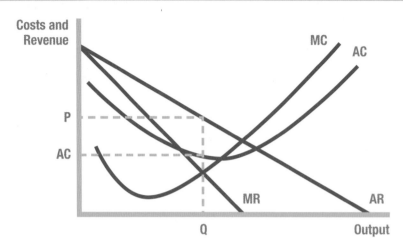

08 | Pros and Cons

Give two advantages and two disadvantages to consumers of a government increasing contestability in markets

Advantage 1	Disadvantage 1
Advantage 2	Disadvantage 2

Give two advantages and two disadvantages to incumbent firms of a government increasing contestability in markets

Advantage 1	Disadvantage 1
Advantage 2	Disadvantage 2

09 | Complete me!

A contestable market is one in which barriers to entry and _____ are very _____, which implies that _____ costs are low. The number of _____ firms in the industry is completely _____; this means that an industry can be contestable with just _____ firm, or many firms. New entrant firms should also have _____ access to the same _____ as incumbent firms. Whilst _____ competitive markets and monopolistically competitive markets are _____ contestable, markets that initially appear to be closer to monopoly or _____ can also be considered contestable, if barriers to entry and exit are low.

Because of the _____ of competition from new firms, incumbent firms are _____ to behave competitively and keep their _____ low. In other words, there does not need to be actual competition for prices to fall, simply the threat of competition. The lowest price that a firm in a contestable market is likely to charge is often known as the _____ price, and is the same as the price at which the firm earns _____ profit. This occurs at the level of output at which _____ revenue is equal to average cost.

Incumbent firms are also often at the mercy of so-called _____ and run competition from new market entrants; new firms are able to quickly and easily enter a market and then leave when they have earned enough profit. This can be particularly damaging to the _____ share of incumbents. Improving contestability is a key pillar of UK government _____ policy.

one	equal	oligopoly	prices
irrelevant	normal	incumbent	low
hit	exit	average	threat
necessarily	sunk	perfectly	technology
competition	limit	incentivised	market

4.1.5.10 MARKET STRUCTURE, STATIC EFFICIENCY, DYNAMIC EFFICIENCY AND RESOURCE ALLOCATION

01 | Define this

Static efficiency	
Dynamic efficiency	

Productive efficiency	
Allocative efficiency	
Human capital	
Non-human capital	

02 | True or False?

Statement	True or False?
Allocative efficiency (providing certain assumptions are met) occurs where price = MC	
Dynamic efficiency is more likely in perfect competition than in industries where firms earn higher profit	
Productive efficiency for the firm occurs where average fixed costs are minimised	
One way in which market structures may be compared is by considering efficiency	
Perfectly competitive firms are always productively efficient	
If a firm is allocatively efficient it must necessarily be productively efficient	
Firms can improve their dynamic efficiency by investing in human capital	

03 | Give me 5!

Give me 5 factors likely to improve dynamic efficiency
1
2
3
4
5

04 | Pros and Cons

Give two advantages and two disadvantages to consumers of a firm achieving productive efficiency

Advantage 1

Disadvantage 1

Advantage 2

Disadvantage 2

Give two advantages and two disadvantages to the wider economy of a firm achieving productive efficiency

Advantage 1

Disadvantage 1

Advantage 2

Disadvantage 2

05 | 3 2 1!

Give me 3 assumptions that must hold for true allocative efficiency to be achieved

1

2

3

Give me 2 benefits of a firm achieving allocative efficiency

1

2

Give me 1 example of a firm that has improved allocative efficiency

1

06 | Draw me!

Draw a diagram to show a perfectly competitive firm operating in the short-run

Is the firm productively efficient?

Is the firm allocatively efficient?

Is the firm dynamically efficient?

Draw a diagram to show a firm in perfect competition in the long run

Is the firm productively efficient?

Is the firm allocatively efficient?

Is the firm dynamically efficient?

Draw a diagram to show a firm in monopolistic competition in the long run

Is the firm productively efficient?

Is the firm allocatively efficient?

Is the firm dynamically efficient?

Draw a diagram to show a firm in monopolistic competition in the short run / a diagram to show a monopoly firm

Is the firm productively efficient?

Is the firm allocatively efficient?

Is the firm dynamically efficient?

Draw a diagram to show a firm in imperfect competition in a highly contestable market, choosing to operate at the normal profit point

Is the firm productively efficient?

Is the firm allocatively efficient?

Is the firm dynamically efficient?

01 | Define this

Consumer surplus	
Producer surplus	
Welfare	
Deadweight loss	

02 | Label me!

The diagram below shows equilibrium in a competitive market.
  i)   Label the area representing consumer surplus
  ii) Label the area representing producer surplus
  iii) Adapt the diagram to show the impact on producer and consumer surplus if the market is now characterised by a monopolist
  iv) Indicate the deadweight welfare loss as a result of the monopoly market structure

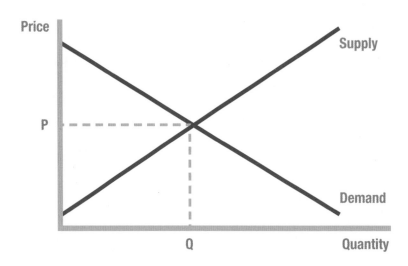

03 | Draw me!

Draw a set of diagrams to show the use of price discrimination by a cinema, in which they charge a different price for adults to students for the same film showing at the same time. Show how consumer and producer change in the price-discriminating situation compared with the non-price-discriminating situation

Please scan the above QR Code to access
the suggested answers for this book.

www.tutor2u.net/economics

AQA | A Level | Economics

SKU: 02-4130-30158-01 |ISBN: 978-1915417411

9781915417411